American Foxho
20 Milestone Challenges

American Foxhound Memorable Moments. Includes
Milestones for Memories, Gifts, Socialization &
Training

Volume 1

Todays Doggy

Copyright © 2019

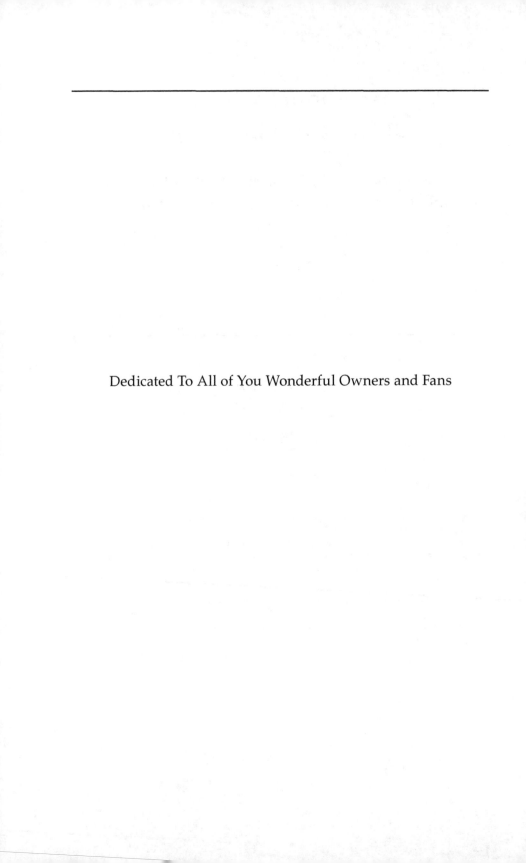

Dedicated To All of You Wonderful Owners and Fans

Introduction

Welcome to the Original Doggy Milestone Series™ where you are encouraged to create those special moments with your dog. We have composed the milestones in a way that challenges you to set the stage before taking your photos.

Use props and make it fun - be creative in setting up your photos. Get family and friends involved - take it out with you - use it in different places and settings - have a play with it and most importantly, have a good time!

You can either hold the desired milestone spread open yourself - or have somebody hold it open as you take the snap.

If you would like to have the selected milestone book spread open and standing independently in your photos, you can use one or two large 'foldback' clips to hold the spread open.

Good luck and enjoy your photo fun.

I Love My Family...

...And My Family Loves Me

At The
Beach!

Having a Wave of a Time

NIGHT

OUT

With My Doggy Pals

IT'S...

BED
TIME

I DIDN'T
KNOW
WHICH
STICK
YOU
THREW

Next Week!

DO
NOT
DISTURB

PLAYING IN THE LEAVES

I Need

a

HUGe

Amount
Of
Treats

Say

ello

OFF

To

The

VET??

CATCH ME IF YOU CAN!

WE'RE A TEAM

NASA

Wants

To Hire

Me

Because
I'm a
STAR!

OOPS!
I
Buried
Your
Stuff

...But I

Forgot

Where

My Real Name Is

SUPER POOCH

Very

Incredible

Pup

I

DIDN'T

DO IT

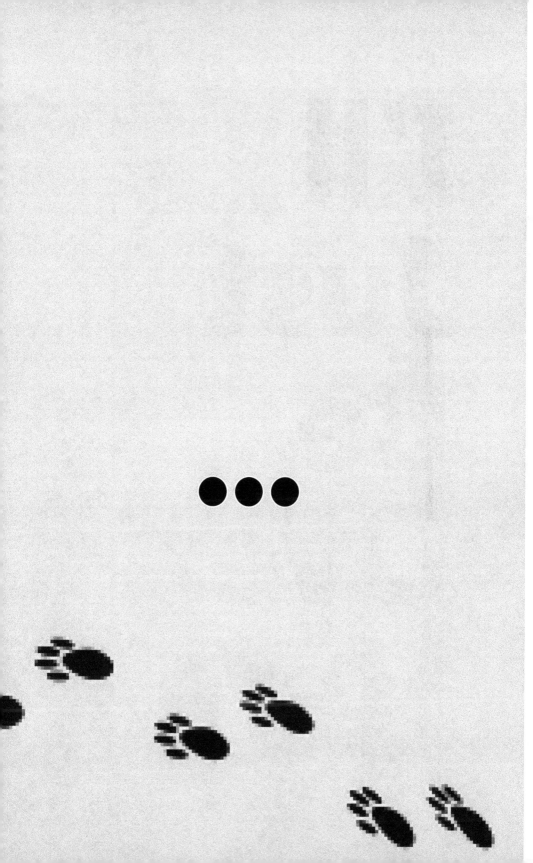

I'll Just Be Over Here...

Looking

Fabulous

PLEASE

PLEASE

PRETTY PLEEEASE

CAN I KEEP IT?

I'm On a SEAFOOD Diet

When
I SEE
FOOD,
I EAT
IT!